THE NOVE

THE NOVEL

WHAT IT IS

BY

F. MARION CRAWFORD

Author of " Mr. Isaacs," " Dr. Claudius," " A Roman
Singer," etc.

GREENWOOD PRESS, PUBLISHERS
WESTPORT, CONNECTICUT

Originally published in 1893
by Macmillan and Company

First Greenwood Reprinting 1970

SBN 8371-2924-9

PRINTED IN UNITED STATES OF AMERICA

WHAT IS A NOVEL?

MY answer can only be a statement of opinion, which I make with much deference to the prejudices of my brethren. Whether it will be of interest to general readers I do not know ; but the question I propose is in itself more or less vital as regards novel-writing. No one will deny that truism. Before going to work it is important to know what one means to do. I pretend, however, to no special gift for solving problems in general or this one in particular. To give " the result of one's experience," as the common

5

phrase puts it, is by no means so easy as it sounds. An intelligent man mostly knows what he means by his own words, but it does not follow that he can convey that meaning to others. Almost all discussion and much misunderstanding may fairly be said to be based upon the difference between the definitions of common terms as understood by the two parties. In the exact sciences there is no such thing as discussion; there is the theorem and its demonstration, there is the problem and its solution, from which solution and demonstration there is no appeal. That is because, in mathematics, every word is defined before it is used and is almost meaningless until it has been defined.

It has been remarked by a very great
authority concerning the affairs of men
that "of making many books there is
no end," and to judge from appear-
ances the statement is even more true
to-day than when it was first made.
Especially of making novels there is
no end, in these times of latter-day
literature. No doubt many wise and
good persons and many excellent critics devoutly wish that there might be ;
but they are not at present strong
enough to stand against us, the army
of fiction-makers, because we are many,
and most of us do not know how to do
anything else, and have grown grey in
doing this particular kind of work, and
are dependent upon it for bread as well
as butter ; and lastly and chiefly, be-

cause we are heavily backed, as a body, by the capital of the publisher, of which we desire to obtain for ourselves as much as possible. Therefore novels will continue to be written, perhaps for a long time to come. There is a demand for them and there is profit in producing them. Who shall prevent us, authors and publishers, from continuing the production and supplying the demand?

This brings with it a first answer to the question, "What is a novel?" A novel is a marketable commodity, of the class collectively termed "luxuries," as not contributing directly to the support of life or the maintenance of health. It is of the class "artistic luxuries" because it does not appeal

to any of the three material senses —
touch, taste, smell; and it is of the
class "intellectual artistic luxuries," because it is not judged by the superior
senses — sight and hearing. The novel,
therefore, is an intellectual artistic luxury — a definition which can be made
to include a good deal, but which is,
in reality, a closer one than it appears
to be at first sight. No one, I think,
will deny that it covers the three principal essentials of the novel as it should
be, of a story or romance, which in
itself and in the manner of telling it
shall appeal to the intellect, shall sat-
isfy the requirements of art, and shall
be a luxury, in that it can be of no use
to a man when he is at work, but may
conduce to peace of mind and delecta-

tion during his hours of idleness. The point upon which people differ is the artistic one, and the fact that such differences of opinion exist makes it possible that two writers as widely separated as Mr. Henry James and Mr. Rider Haggard, for instance, find appreciative readers in the same year of the same century—a fact which the literary history of the future will find it hard to explain.

PROBABLY no one denies that the first object of the novel is to amuse and interest the reader. But it is often said that the novel should instruct as well as afford amusement, and the " novel-with-a-purpose " is the realisation of this idea. We might invent a better expression than that clumsy translation of the neat German *"Tendenz-Roman."* Why not compound the words and call the odious thing a " purpose-novel "? The purpose-novel, then, proposes to serve two masters, besides procuring a reasonable amount of bread and butter for its writer and publisher. It proposes to escape from my definition of the novel in general and make itself an " intellectual moral lesson " instead of an " intellectual artistic luxury." It constitutes a violation of the unwritten contract tacitly existing between writer and reader. So far as supply and demand are concerned, books in general and works of fiction in particular are commodities and subject to the same laws, statutory and traditional, as other articles of manufacture. A toy-dealer would not venture to sell real pistols to little boys as pop-guns, and a gun-maker who should try to sell the latter for army revolvers would get into trouble, even though he were able to prove that the toy was as expensive to manufacture as the real article, or more so, silver-

mounted, chiselled, and lying in a
Russia-leather case.   I am not sure
that the law might not support the
purchaser in an action for damages if
he discovered at a critical moment
that his revolver was a plaything.   It
seems to me that there is a similar case
in the matter of novels.   A man buys
what purports to be a work of fiction, a
romance, a novel, a story of adventure,
pays his money, takes his book home,
prepares to enjoy it at his ease, and
discovers that he has paid a dollar for
somebody's views on socialism, religion,
or the divorce laws.

Such books are generally carefully
suited with an attractive title.   The
binding is as frivolous as can be de-
sired.   The bookseller says it is " a

work of great power," and there is
probably a sentimental dedication on
the fly-leaf to a number of initials to
which a romantic appearance is given
by the introduction of a stray " St."
and a few hyphens. The buyer is
possibly a conservative person, of luke-
warm religious convictions, whose life
is made "barren by marriage, or death,
or division " — and who takes no sort
of interest in the laws relating to divorce, in the invention of a new religion,
or the position of the labour question.
He has simply paid money, on the
ordinary tacit contract between fur-
nisher and purchaser, and he has been
swindled, to use a very plain term for
which a substitute does not occur to
me. Or say that a man buys a seat

in one of the regular theatres. He
enters, takes his place, preparing to be
amused, and the curtain goes up. The
stage is set as a church, there is a
pulpit before the prompter's box, and
the Right Reverend the Bishop of the
Diocese is on the point of delivering
a sermon. The man would be legally
justified in demanding his money at
the door, I fancy, and would probably
do so, though he might admit that
the Bishop was the most learned and
edifying of preachers. There are indeed certain names and prefixes to
names which suggest serious reading,
independently of the words printed on
the title-page of the book. If the
Archbishop of Canterbury, or General
Booth, or the Emperor William pub-

lished a novel, for instance, the work might reasonably be expected to contain an exposition of personal views on some question of the day. But in ordinary cases the purpose-novel is a simple fraud, besides being a failure in nine hundred and ninety-nine cases out of a thousand.

What we call a novel may educate the taste and cultivate the intelligence; under the hand of genius it may purify the heart and fortify the mind; it should never under any circumstances be suffered to deprave the one nor to weaken the other; it may stand for scores of years — and a score of years is a long time in our day — as the exposition of all that is noble, heroic, honest, and true in the life of woman

or man ; but it has no right to tell us
what its writer thinks about the rela-
tions of labour and capital, nor to set
up what the author conceives to be a
nice, original, easy scheme of salvation,
any more than it has a right to take
for its theme the relative merits of the
" broomstick-car " and the " storage
system," temperance, vivisection, or the
"Ideal Man" of Confucius. Lessons,
lectures, discussions, sermons, and di-
dactics generally belong to institutions
set apart for especial purposes and
carefully avoided, after a certain age,
by the majority of those who wish to
be amused. The purpose-novel is an
odious attempt to lecture people who
hate lectures, to preach at people who
prefer their own church, and to teach

people who think they know enough already. It is an ambush, a lying-in-wait for the unsuspecting public, a violation of the social contract — and as such it ought to be either mercilessly crushed or forced by law to bind itself in black and label itself " Purpose " in very big letters.

IN art of all kinds the moral lesson
is a mistake. It is one thing to ex-
hibit an ideal worthy to be imitated,
though inimitable in all its perfection,
but so clearly noble as to appeal directly to the sympathetic string that
hangs untuned in the dullest human
heart; to make man brave without
arrogance, woman pure without prud-
ishness, love enduring yet earthly, not
angelic, friendship sincere but not
ridiculous. It is quite another matter
to write a "guide to morality" or a
"hand-book for practical sinners" and
call either one a novel, no matter how
much fiction it may contain. Words-

worth tried the moral lesson and spoiled
some of his best work with botany
and the Bible. A good many smaller
men than he have tried the same
thing since, and have failed. Perhaps
" Cain " and " Manfred " have taught
the human heart more wisdom than
" Matthew " or the unfortunate " idiot
boy " over whom Byron was so mercilessly merry. And yet Byron probably
never meant to teach any one anything
in particular, and Wordsworth meant
to teach everybody, including and beginning with himself.

There are, I believe, two recognised
ways of looking at art : art for the public or " art for art," to adopt the current
French phrase. Might we not say, Art
for the buyer and art for the seller?

Or is that too practical a view to take
of what is supposed to be so eminently
unpractical as art itself ? Has it not
been said similarly, and with truth, that
religion is for man, and not man for
religion? Is it our province to please
those who read our works, or to force
them to please us by buying them?
Do not these questions lie at the root
of the conflict between realism and
romance? Are we to take Talleyrand's
speech as our guide? — "I have fur-
nished you with an argument ; I am not
bound to furnish you with an understanding." The story is old, but the
position it defines is as old as humanity.
When a novelist turns prophet, it will
be time enough for him to convert his
readers at the point of the pen. Are

we writers so vain as a class, and so proud of ourselves as men, as to be above affording amusement to our readers without attempting to comfort them, to teach or to preach to them? We are not poets, because we cannot be. We are not genuine playwriters for many reasons; chiefly, perhaps, because we are not clever enough, since a successful play is incomparably more lucrative than a successful novel. We are not preachers, and few of us would be admitted to the pulpit. We are not, as a class, teachers or professors, nor lawyers, nor men of business. We are nothing more than public amusers. Unless we choose we need not be anything less. Let us, then, accept our position cheerfully, and do

the best we can to fulfil our mission,
without attempting to dignify it with
titles too imposing for it to bear, and
without degrading it by bringing its
productions down even a little way,
from the lowest level of high comedy
to the highest level of buffoonery. It
is good to make people laugh; it is
sometimes salutary to make them shed
tears; it is best of all to make our
readers think — not too serious thoughts,
nor such as require an intimate knowledge of science and philosophy to be
called thoughts at all — but to think,
and, thinking, to see before them characters whom they might really like to
resemble, acting in scenes in which
they themselves would like to take
a part. In trying to amuse, let us

be consistent each in his own way,
never giving our public a pretext of
appealing from Philip drunk to Philip
sober. If we have poetry within us,
let us put such of it as is worth anything into our books, for almost all
poetry which deserves the name is
good. But let us keep out of our
novels all that savours of preaching and
teaching, for our readers' sakes; and
for our own, all such matter as is
limited by modern science, present
fashion, and actual taste, and which
consequently imposes too wilful a
limitation upon the permanence of
our own work.

B^{UT} I perceive that although this little essay is not a work of fiction, I myself am falling into one of the errors which I have wished to point out, for I am beginning to preach where I have no right to inculcate a lesson, and mean only to express a purely personal opinion in the only matter upon which a novelist is justified in expressing one at all. Moreover, I hereby disclaim all intention of setting an example, since in many points upon which I have touched I admit that I myself am the last of literary sinners; and with this admission of fallibility and confession of weakness I cry *peccavi*, and ask absolution of the public.

I do not wish to be accused of what is called smart writing. It is much easier to attack than to defend and much more blessed to give hard knocks than to receive them. A professed novelist is perhaps not a competent judge of novels from the point of view which interests the reader, and which is of course the reader's own. We know the *technique* of the trick better than the effect it produces, just as it is hard for a conjuror to realise the sensations of the old gentleman in the audience who finds a bowl of goldfish in his waistcoat pocket. We do not all know one another's tricks, but we have a fair idea of the general principle on which they are done and a very definite opinion about our own business as compared with that of the parson or the professor. We know our books from the inside and we see the strings of the puppets, while the public only guesses at the mechanism as it sits before the stage, watching the marionettes and listening to the voice from behind the scenes. A novel is, after all, a play, and perhaps it is nothing but a substitute for the real play with live characters, scene-shifting, and footlights. But miracle-plays have gone out of fashion in modern times, except at Ober-Ammergau. The purpose-novel is a miracle-play — and if it be true that any really good novel can be dramatised, nothing short of a miracle could put a purpose-novel on the boards.

Most people have a very clear conception of what a good play ought to be, and of the precise extent to which realism can be effective without being offensive. But it is strange, and it is a bad sign of the times, that persons who would not tolerate a coarse play read novels little, if at all, short of indecent. An answer suggests itself which may be comprehensive as an explanation, but is insufficient as an excuse. In our Anglo-Saxon social system the young girl is everywhere, and, if the shade of Sterne will allow me to say so, we temper the wind of our realism to the sensitive innocence of the ubiquitous shorn lamb. Once

admit that the young girl is to have the
freedom of our theatre, and it follows,
and ought to follow, and very generally
does follow, that our plays must be
suited to maiden ears and eyes. It is
a good thing that this should be so,
but the effect is rather strange. The
men who hear plays in English are
not, perhaps, more moral than their
contemporaries of Paris, Vienna, and
Berlin. We like to believe that our
women are better than those of foreign
nations. We owe it to them to put
more faith in them because they are
our own, our dear mothers and wives
and sisters and daughters, for whom, if
we be men, we mean to do all that
men can do. But we are all men and
women nevertheless, and human, and

we have the thoughts and the understanding of men and women and not of
school-girls. Yet the school-girl practically decides what we are to hear at
the theatre and, so far as our own
language is concerned, determines to a
great extent what we are to read.

But if we do not write for the young
girl, who will? We have not the ad-
vantage possessed by the French of
satisfying the demands of young people
by translations from works in other
languages. The young girl in France,
as a matter of fact, reads Walter Scott,
Bulwer, and Dickens, while her mother
diverts her leisure with the more lively
productions of Paul Bourget, Guy de
Maupassant, or possibly Balzac, whom
all educated Frenchmen and French-

women are at least supposed to have read. The advocate of a broader license in the English fiction of the future may answer that the whole body of novels already in existence should be more than sufficient for the delectation of "the young." Should the development of the new school, however, lead to the creation of a literature in our language, resembling, as a whole, that of the French, our novel, in its present form, would soon cease to be written, and those of the type which are already in existence would in a short time be regarded as antiquated, dull, and savouring of the Sunday-school. Youth, too, dislikes to be treated as youth. The old, who regretfully long to be young again, may find

some consolation in the ardent desire
of youth for mature years. Moreover,
it is easier to lower the reader's moral
tone than to raise it ever so little.
The ambition of all boys, and probably
of very many young girls, is to read
such novels as their parents do not
habitually leave on the drawing-room
table. Every boy wants to read " Guy
Livingstone," and most boys do, with
or without their mamma's permission,
at a very early age. If we advanced
so far as the French realistic point of
view, that book would become a common property of boys and girls, and
perhaps " Nana," or " Les Mensonges,"
would take its place in the estimation
of our children, — a consummation
devoutly to be prayed against. Our

" books for the young " are not, on the whole, a success, unless we are willing to modify the expression, and call them books for the very young. There are not in existence, I believe, enough really interesting, and yet perfectly harmless, novels to occupy the vast amount of spare time which the young seem ready to devote to literature, and which we, the workers, seek in vain. It is not always easy to see — it is certainly not easy for us to explain — why we novelists occasionally introduce a thought, a page, or a chapter in a novel otherwise fit for a child's ears, which may have the effect, so to say, of turning weak tea into bad whiskey. Yet most of us have done it, contemplate doing it, or at least go so far as to wish that we might allow ourselves the liberty.   Perhaps, if that liberty were universally granted, we should desire it less.   Perhaps a number of my colleagues will not admit that they desire it at all.   I believe that in most cases it is only a desire to escape from limitations not unlike those overstepped when an author writes much in dialect. It looks as though it might be easier to write interesting books with the help of the knowledge of evil, as well as with the help of the knowledge of good ; and after a certain number of years of hard work a novelist instinctively leans towards any method of lightening his labours which presents itself to his tired imagination.   If he yields once, he will probably yield again

and fall into the slipshod, careless ways
for which the overworked man is often
cruelly, if not altogether unjustly,
blamed. For the public, which most
of us acknowledge to be a perfectly
just body in the long run, is as thor-
oughly unforgiving as Justice herself.
" He has written himself out." How
carelessly that little phrase is often
uttered ! How terrible it is for any
author to hear ! It is indeed a solemn
memento mori, the phrase of all others
of which we dread the application to
ourselves. For the romance of ro-
mancing soon disappears. After the
production of one, two, three, or half-
a-dozen novels, if the writer is really
what we call " a professional," and
must go on writing as a business, he

discovers how serious is the occupation
in which he is engaged.   Half-a-dozen
books, or less, will make a reputation ;
ten will sustain one ; twenty are in
ordinary cases a career.   Does any
one, not an author, who reads these
lines guess at the labour, the imagination, the industry, the set purpose, the
courage, which are necessary to produce
a score of novels of an average good
quality?   And if not, how can he
understand the intense longing for a
removal of restraint, for a little more
liberty that tempts the overwrought
intelligence into error?   Far be it
from me to appeal in any way to the
public pity, for my own sake or in be-
half of others.   We are no more to be
pitied when we break down than an old

shoemaker who can no longer see the
point of his bristles, and not so much
as a broken-winded cab-horse that has
never had any option in the choice of
a career. Let this be taken as an
explanation, not as an apology. To
judge from the standards of some people, however, the worn-out novelist,
whose works have filled the shelves of
the young girl of the period, might
find profitable employment if he would
adopt the tenets of realism and write
for the jaded taste of those who,
whether already old or what is called
still young, have exhausted their capac-
ity for bread and milk and crave red
pepper and stimulants.

The taste for " realism " is abroad,
and in opposition to all this. Out

of the conflict arises that very curious production, the realistic novel in English — than which no effort of human genius has sailed nearer to the wind, so to say, since Goethe wrote his " Elective Affinities," which an Anglo-Saxon young girl pronounced to be " a dull book all about gardening." That our prevailing moral literary purity is to some extent assumed — not fictitious — is shown by the undeniable fact that women who blush scarlet, and men who feel an odd sensation of repulsion in reading some pages of " Tom Jones " or " Peregrine Pickle," are not conscious of any particular shock when their sensibilities are attacked in French. Some of them call Zola a " pig " with great direct-

ness, but read all his books indus-
triously, and very often admit the fact.
When they call him names they forget that he writes for a great public
of men and women, not for young girls
— and when they read him he makes
them remember that he is a great man
— mistaken perhaps, possibly bad,
mightily coarse to no purpose, but
great nevertheless — a Nero of fiction.
But Zola's shadow, seen through the
veil of the English realistic novel, is
a monstrosity not to be tolerated. We
see the apparent contradiction in our
own taste between our theory and our
practice in reading, but we feel instinctively that there is a foundation of
justice to account for the seeming dis-
crepancy. Both are coarse, but the

one is great and bold, and the other is damned by its own smallness and meanness. The result of the desire for realism in men who try to write realistic novels for the clean-minded American and English girl is unsatisfactory. It is generally a photograph, not a picture — a catalogue, not a description.

A community of vices is a closer and more direct bond between human beings than a community of virtues. This may be because vice needs solidarity among those who yield to it in order to be tolerated at all, whereas virtue is its own reward, as the proverb says, and is happily very often its own protection — far more often than not, in our day. This seems to be the rea-

son why the realistic method is better
suited to the exposition of what is bad
than of what is good. Wordsworth
and Swinburne are two realistic poets.
Most people do not hesitate to call
Wordsworth the greater man. I need
not express an opinion which few
would care to hear, but so far as the
relative effect of their work is concerned it can hardly be denied that,
of the two, Swinburne appeals far more
strongly and directly to sinful humanity as it is. Wordsworth speaks to the
higher and more spiritual part of us,
indeed, but too often in language
which rouses no response in the more
human side of man's nature which is
most generally uppermost. These are
but illustrations of my meaning, not

examples, which latter should be taken among novelists — a task, however, which may be left to the discriminating reader.

IT has always seemed to me that the perfect novel, as it ought to be, exists somewhere in the state of the Platonic idea, waiting to be set down on paper by the first man of genius who receives a direct literary inspiration. It must deal chiefly with love; for in that passion all men and women are most generally interested, either for its present reality, or for the memories that soften the coldly vivid recollection of an active past, and shed a tender light in the dark places of bygone struggles, or because the hope of it brightens and gladdens the path of future dreams. The perfect novel must be clean and sweet, for it must tell its tale to all mankind, to saint and sinner, pure and defiled, just and unjust. It must have the magic to fascinate and the power to hold its reader from first to last. Its realism must be real, of three dimensions, not flat and photographic; its romance must be of the human heart and truly human, that is, of the earth as we all have found it; its idealism must be transcendent, not measured to man's mind, but proportioned to man's soul. Its religion must be of such grand and universal span as to hold all worthy religions in itself. Conceive, if possible, such a story, told in language that can be now simple, now keen, now passionate, and now sublime — or rather, pray, do not conceive it, for the modern novelist's occupation would suddenly be gone, and that one book would stand alone of its kind, making all others worse than useless — ridiculous, if not sacrilegious, by comparison.

Why must a novel-writer be either a "realist" or a "romantist"? And, if the latter, why "romanticist" any more than "realisticist"? Why should a good novel not combine romance and reality in just proportions? Is there any reason to suppose that the one element must necessarily shut out the other? Both are included in every-day life, which would be a very dull affair without something of the one, and would be decidedly incoherent without the other. Art, if it is "to create and foster agreeable illusions," as Napoleon is believed to have said of it, should represent the real, but in such a way as to make it seem more agreeable and interesting than it actually is. That is the only way to create "an agreeable illusion," and by no other means can a novel do good while remaining a legitimate novel and not becoming a sermon, a treatise, or a polemic.

It may reasonably be inquired whether the prevailing and still growing taste for fiction expresses a new and enduring want of educated men and women. The novel, as we understand the word, is after all a very recent invention. Considering that we do not find it in existence until late in the last century, its appearance must be admitted to

have been very sudden, its growth
fabulously rapid, and its development
enormous. The ancients had nothing
more like it than a few collections of
humorous and pathetic stories. The
Orientals, who might be supposed to
feel the need of it even more than we
do, had nothing but their series of fantastic tales strung rather loosely together without general plan. Men and
women seem to have survived the dul-
ness of the dark age with the help of
the itinerant story-teller. The novel is
a distinctly modern invention, satisfying a modern want. In the ideal state
described with so much accuracy by
Mr. Bellamy, I believe the novel would
not sell. It would be incomprehensible,
or it would not be a novel at all, ac-

cording to our understanding. Do away practically with the struggle for life, eliminate all the unfit and make the surviving fittest perfectly comfortable — men and women might still take a curious interest in our present civilisation, but it would be of a purely historical nature. To gratuitously invent a tale of a poor man fighting for success would seem to them a piece of monstrously bad taste and ridiculously useless. Are we tending to such a state as that? There are those who believe that we are — but a faith able to remove mountains at "cut rates" will not be more than enough to realise their hopes.

IT may fairly be claimed that humanity has, within the past hundred years, found a way of carrying a theatre in its pocket; and so long as humanity remains what it is, it will delight in taking out its pocket-stage and watching the antics of the actors, who are so like itself and yet so much more interesting. Perhaps that is, after all, the best answer to the question, "What is a novel?" It is, or ought to be, a pocket-stage. Scenery, light, shade, the actors themselves, are made of words, and nothing but words, more or less cleverly put together. A play is good in proportion as it represents

the more dramatic, passionate, romantic, or humorous sides of real life. A
novel is excellent according to the
degree in which it produces the illusions of a good play — but it must not
be forgotten that the play is the thing,
and that illusion is eminently necessary
to success.

Every writer who has succeeded has
his own methods of creating such illusion. Some of us are found out, and
some of us are not; but we all do the
same thing in one way or another, con-
sciously or unconsciously. The tricks
of the art are without number, simple
or elaborate, easily learned or hard to
imitate, and many of us consider that
we have a monopoly of certain tricks
we call our own, and are unreasonably

angry when a competitor makes use of them.

The means, all subservient to language, are many, but the object is always one : to make the reader realise as far as possible the writer's conception of his story.

That word "realise" has a greater value and a wider application upon the question which I am endeavouring to treat so briefly than in ordinary conversation. To realise means to make real from one's own standpoint, to see as vividly through the imagination what is partially imaginary as what is altogether imagined ; in other words, to call up an image as coincident with the representations of fact as truth itself. Of course, in a printed book, the author has no means to attain this end excepting language, and upon the terms of language employed must depend a very large part of his success. Language is the tool with which he makes his weapons, and these in their turn may vary in manufacture and temper according to his requirements. The most powerful weapon of all is what is most commonly called truth to nature. Goethe said of his "Wilhelm Meister," "there is nothing in it which I have not lived and nothing exactly as I lived it"; yet most people would call "Wilhelm Meister" a fantastic book. Other means of producing an impression are local colour, the use of dialects and foreign languages. Here I know I am touching upon a very delicate point, and that I risk wounding the sensibilities of many writers and attacking the individual tastes of many readers of fiction. Nevertheless, the mention of the dialect-novel raises a question which is before the literary grand jury of the world. Assuredly every man has a prime right to make use of the material at his disposal; and if some particular dialect forms a part of this stock in trade, he is as free to employ it as an African traveller, for instance, is free to introduce his own reminiscences into a novel, if he writes one. Colour alone amuses some people, chiefly children. Small boys and girls do not despise a kaleidoscope as a toy on a rainy day, and dialect without dramatic interest is colour without form or outline, and some novels in dialect are nothing more. But then, there are plenty of works of fiction written in ordinary English which have not even that one merit, and of these I do not wish to say anything. Take a really good novel, however, in which more than half the pages are filled with dialogues in a language not familiar to the English-speaking public as a whole. Is not the writer wilfully limiting his audience, if not himself? Is he not sacrificing his privilege of addressing all men, for the sake of addressing a few in terms which they especially prefer? Is he not preferring local popularity to broader and more enduring reputation? Could he not, by the skilful use of description, by a clever handling of grammar and a careful selection of words, produce an impression which should be more widely felt, though less warmly received, perhaps, in that one small public to which he appeals? Is he not, although he be a first-rate man, often tempted to lapses of literary conscience by the peculiar facilities he finds in the literary by-way he has chosen? How much of what is screaming farce in the dialect of the few, would be funny if translated into plain English for the many? Wit and humour are intellectual, and when genuine are susceptible of being translated into almost all languages; but dialect seems to me to rank with puns, and with puns of a particular local character. A practical demonstration of this is found in the fact that stories in dialect, when told and not read, are duller than any other stories, unless the teller has the power of imitating accents. Almost all limitations which a man willingly assumes afford facilities for the sake of which he assumes them.

BUT this is not the place for a study of methods. So far as I have been able, I have answered the question I asked, and which stands at the head of this essay. But I have answered it in my own way. What am I, a novel-writer, trying to do? I am trying, with such limited means as I have at my disposal, to make little pocket-theatres out of words. I am trying to be architect, scene-painter, upholsterer, drama-tist and stage-manager, all at once. Is it any wonder if we novelists do not succeed as well as we could wish, when we try to be masters of so many trades?

Nor is this all. The great development of the modern superficial education in society has brought with it a thirst for knowledge which adds considerably to the difficulties of the novelist's art. There are few sciences, few of the arts, few of the branches of learning, in which the reading public does not take some sort of interest. That interest is not a profound one, but with its growth encyclopædias, primers, and "cram-books" have multiplied exceedingly on the face of the earth. Upon the slightest suspicion the reader accuses the author of inaccuracy, goes to his own, or his friend's, or the Public Library's bookshelves, takes down the "Encyclopædia Britannica," the "Century Dictionary,"

or "Larousse," and with cruel direct-
ness sets the author right. We are
expected to be omniscient, to understand the construction of the telephone,
the latest theories concerning the chol-
era microbe, the mysteries of hypno-
tism, the Russian language, and the
nautical dictionary. We are supposed
to be intimately acquainted with the
writings of Macrobius, the music of
Wagner, and the Impressionist school
of painting. In these days when there
has been much discussion concerning
the authorship of Shakespeare's plays,
— concerning which "Punch" wisely
said they were probably written by
another man of the same name, —
the principal argument against Bacon's
authorship of them seems to me to be

this : No one man of whom we have ever known anything can be conceived capable of having produced such an enormous body of thoughtful work as is contained in what is attributed to Shakespeare and in what is known to have been written by Bacon. And yet, for the sake of a little profit and the inducement of a modicum of glory, we authors are sometimes expected to rival both. The absurdity of this is apparent to the most ordinary mind and painfully so to the ordinary critic, who, though he may never have written a book, may very possibly know more than we do about some subjects upon which we are obliged to write. Dr. Johnson, it will be remembered, said that a man need not be a coach-builder in order to say that a carriage is well made. I am aware that many persons will think my statement exaggerated, or, if they do not, will say that they prefer an honest love story to a tale involving the intricacies of the modern invention. And I believe there has been a reaction in this respect. With regard to the play, it is the opinion of some of the best actors and most successful managers now alive, that the public, if it really knew what it wanted, instead of being forced to feed upon what it gets, would demand real, old-fashioned love pieces rather than comedies, dramas and melodramas, in which the leading actor is the mechanician and the hero of the piece is little more than a " walking gentleman." On my theory that the novel is, or should be, a play, the same must be approximately true about fiction. An acquaintance with the developments of modern science cannot do more than lend a modern colour to the story, and so far as that goes the more closely acquainted we are with such things, the better for us. But no one has a right to demand that we should know everything, in order to find fault with us if we lose our heads over the reversing gear of a locomotive or the most approved fashion of rigging a top-gallant studding-sail boom.

One may be pardoned for asking sometimes whether the advance of science does not almost mean the retreat of thought. Again I protest against trifles as dresses, ruffles — or fire-engines for the emotions they excited in the hearts of their listeners.

the accusation of smart writing, which is so easily brought, so hard to bear, and so difficult to refute. I do not mean that science thinks less as she progresses, but I do mean to say that there is much in favour of the *homo unius libri* — the man of one book — the man who reads less and thinks more than his fellows. The wonders of science are very attractive, many of them are decidedly spectacular and may be used by the author to amuse when he cannot interest, but I doubt whether books which depend upon them for success will be much more popular fifty years hence than "Sandford and Merton" or Paley's "Evidences of Christianity" are in our time. At that not distant future date, our grandchildren will probably look upon our quoted wonders and marvels with about as much interest as we regard the experiment of asphyxiating a mouse under the receiver of an air-pump, or making a piece of paper stick to a piece of rubbed sealing-wax and explaining that it is electricity. Yet, to take an instance, medicine and surgery play a considerable part in modern light literature, and the fire-engine is a distinct feature on the modern stage. Generally speaking, I venture to say that anything which fixes the date of the novel not intended to be historical is a mistake, from a literary point of view. It is not wise to describe the cut of the hero's coat, nor the draping of the heroine's gown, the shape of her hat, nor the colour of his

tie. Ten years hence somebody may buy the book and turn up his nose at "those times." Until a date which may still be called recent, it was customary to play Shakespeare with the dress of modern times. Garrick, I think, played Macbeth in a full bottomed wig. I may be wrong, bu I have the impression that what v call stage costume first became co mon in his days and to some exten his individual efforts. In Shakesp times, Achilles in "Troilus and sida" dressed like Sir Walter F and Cymbeline perhaps lik VIII., to give himself a antiquity. But there wa absurd about the plays for cause they did not depen

THE danger of falling into absurdities
lies not in anachronisms of dress,
but in speeches that contradict sentiments, and actions that belie the character. We need not go far to find truth,
but having begun our search in one di-
rection, we must not wander to another,
or we shall fall out of the natural se-
quence of events upon which we depend
for the effect of reality. For a man of
superior gifts there is an easy but dangerous way out of the difficulty. Instead of inventing his characters he may
take men and women who have really
lived and played parts in the world's
story and have made love, so to say, in

the face of all humanity. In other words, he may write an historical novel.

The historical novel occupies a position apart and separate from others, but it does not follow that it should not conform exactly to the conditions required of an ordinary work of fiction, though it must undoubtedly possess other qualities peculiar to itself. It is doubtful whether any genuine historical novel has ever yet been written for the sake of the history it contains. In nine cases out of ten the writer has selected his subject because it interests him, because it has dramatic elements, and possibly because he hopes to interest his readers more readily by means of characters and events altogether beyond the reach of the carping critic. If this is not the case, it is hard indeed to see why the historical novel should be written at all, seeing that it is neither fish, flesh, nor fowl, but salad. It is indeed a regrettable fact, but also an indubitable one, that a good many people of our time have derived their knowledge of French history from the novels of Alexandre Dumas, and of some of the most important events in the story of the British Empire from those of Walter Scott. But no one pretends that such books are history deserving to be taught as such, and the writers certainly made no such pretensions themselves. Where fact and fiction are closely linked together, the elements may obviously be mixed in an infinite variety, and in any possible degree of relative intensity —

all wine and no water, or almost all
water and no wine to speak of. Pro-
vided that no attempt is made to palm
off the historical novel as a school-book,
there can be no real objection to it on
other grounds.

It seems quite certain that the oldest
form of dramatic art dealt solely with
subjects considered at the time to be
historical, or which constituted articles of belief. The Greek dramatists
founded all their plays, without excep-
tion, so far as I know, upon history,
myths, or traditions, either religious or
secular, and produced works of un-
rivalled beauty and enduring strength.
Some one once called the novel the
" modern epic." There is just enough
truth in the saying to give it social

currency in conversation, but it is true, so far as we know, that the ancient epic preceded the ancient drama, creating the taste and the demand for emotions which the dramatists subsequently satisfied, and it was perhaps because the epic was wholly historical in a measure, that the drama was founded upon an historical basis. The average novelist likes to make use of historical facts principally because he knows that his critics cannot impugn the possibility of the situations he uses, while the latter are so strong in themselves as to bear the burden of the writer's faults with comparative ease, if his talents are not remarkable. If he is a man of genius, he gets a certain amount of very valuable liberty by doing his "sensation work " with tragic facts widely known, which help to produce in the reader's mind an *a priori* impression of interest, perfectly legitimate because perfectly well grounded, but enormously in the writer's favour.   Altogether there is much to be said for the historical novel, if we take the view that the novel itself is but a portable play ; and there is no especial reason why we should be so desperately true to the definitions of common parlance as to say that the novel must be a work of fiction and nothing else.   But in the case of the historical novel there is a very important proviso which must never be forgotten under any circumstances.   It must be good.   The ordinary story may be bad from an artistic point of view, and may nevertheless succeed as a literary speculation; but in treating of history, where the personages are great and the events are of stupendous import, the distance which separates the sublime from the ridiculous is even less than the step to which Tom Payne limited it. No author can make Julius Cæsar, Mary Stuart, or Louis XIV ridiculous; but no writer should forget that they can make a laughing-stock of him in his book almost as easily as they could have done in real life. On the whole, therefore, the historical novel is always likely to prove more dangerous to the writer than to the reader, since, when it fails to be a great book, it will in all likelihood be an absurd one. For historical facts are

limitations, and he who subjects himself to them must be willing to under-
take all the responsibility they imply.
Nothing is easier than to write a fantastic tale against which no criticism
can be brought beyond a vague statement that it is dull or worthless, and
not worth reading; but so soon as a
man deals with events which have
actually taken place, he is bounded on
all sides by a multitude of details with
which he must be acquainted and from
which he cannot escape. I have sometimes wondered whether Walter Savage
Landor did not really meditate writing
an historical novel at some time during
the evolution of the " Imaginary Conver-
sations." More than one work of the
kind, and assuredly of the highest order,

must have presented itself to his mind, since he possessed in a supreme degree the power most necessary to the historical novelist, that of seizing the dramatic points in the lives of historical personages and of creating splendid dramatic dialogues without at any time compromising undoubted facts. In other words, he knew how to combine the romantic and the real in such true and just proportions as to demonstrate clearly that they may and should go hand in hand. And this brings us back to the great question of romance and realism, two words which can hardly fail to drop from the modern writer's pen in treating of such a subject.

THERE is much talk in our day of the realistic school of fiction, and the romantic school, though not often mentioned, is understood to be opposed to it. Of course, it is easy to enter into a long discussion about the exact meanings of the two words; but, on the whole, it seems to be true that if the people who talk about schools of fiction mean anything or wish to mean anything, which sometimes seems doubtful, they mean this: the realist proposes to show men what they are; the romantist tries to show men what they should be. It is very unlikely that mankind will ever agree as to the relative merits of these two, and the discussion which was practically begun in Plato's time is not likely to end so long as people care what they read or what they think. The most any one can do is to give a personal opinion, and that means, of course, that he who expresses it commits himself and publicly takes either the one side or the other. For my part, I believe that more good can be done by showing men what they may be, ought to be, or can be, than by describing their greatest weaknesses with the highest art. We all know how bad we are; but it needs much encouragement to persuade some of us to believe that we can really be any better. To create genuine interest, and afford rest and

legitimate amusement, without losing
sight of that fact, and to do so in a
more or less traditional way, seems to
be the profession of the novelist who
belongs to the romantic persuasion.

That novel-writing is a business I am
credibly informed by my publishers.
And since that is the case, it must be
taken for granted that it is a business
which to some extent must be practised
like any other and which will succeed
or fail in the hands of any particular
man according as he is more or less
fitted to carry it on. The qualifications
for any business are three : native talent, education, and industry. Where
there is success of the right kind, the
talent and power of application must
be taken for granted. The education

is and always must be a question of cir-
cumstance.   With regard to novel-writing, when I speak of education I am
not referring to it in the ordinary sense.
Some people take a great deal of interest in concrete things, while others care
more for humanity.   The education of
a novelist is the experience of men and
women which he has got at first hand
in the course of his own life, for he is
of that class to whom humanity offers a
higher interest than inanimate nature.
He can use nature and art only as a
scene and background upon which and
before which his personages move and
have their being.   It is his business
to present his readers with something
which I have called the pocket-theatre,
something which every man may carry

in his pocket, believing that he has only to open it in order to look in upon the theatre of the living world. To produce it, to prepare it, to put it into a portable and serviceable shape, the writer must know what that living world is, what the men in it do and what the women think, why women shed tears and children laugh and young men make love and old men repeat themselves. While he is writing his book, his human beings must be with him, before him, moving before the eye of his mind and talking into the ear of his heart. He must have lived himself; he must have loved, fought, suffered, and struggled in the human battle. I would almost say that to describe another's death he must himself have died.

All this accounts perhaps for the fact that readers are many and writers few. The reader knows one side of life, his own, better than the writer possibly can, and he reads with the greatest interest those books which treat of lives like his own. But the writer must have seen and known many phases of existence, and this is what the education of the novelist means : to know and understand, so far as he is able, men and women who have been placed in unusual circumstances. And this need not and should not lead him into creating altogether imaginary characters, nor men and women whose circumstances are not only unusual, but altogether impossible. We see grotesque pieces given at the theatre

— too grotesque and too often given
— which make us laugh, but never
make us think. They would not make
good novels. The novel must amuse,
indeed, but should amuse reasonably,
from an intellectual point of view,
rather than as a piece of good fun.
Its object is to make one see men and
women who might really live, talk, and
act as they do in the book, and some
of whom one would perhaps like to
imitate. Its intention is to amuse and
please, and certainly not to teach or
preach; but in order to amuse well it
must be a finely-balanced creation,
neither hysterical with tears nor con-
vulsed with perpetual laughter. The
one is as tiring as the other and, in the
long run, as unnatural.

IT is easy, comparatively speaking, to appeal to the emotions, but it is hard to appeal to the heart. This may sound somewhat contradictory at first, but there is truth in it, nevertheless. The outward emotions are in real life much more the expressions of the temperament than of what we call the heart. We all know that there are men and women who laugh and cry more easily than others, and we are rather inclined to believe that these are not they who feel most deeply. A very difficult question here presents itself. Bacon says somewhere that we are apt to extol the powers of the human intellect without invoking its aid as often as we might. This extolling of humanity has been a fashion of late years, and it has not yet disappeared, though its popularity is waning fast. In England Sir Andrew Clarke, M.D., has recently talked learnedly of "the religion of the body," and Lord Coleridge with eloquence of "the religion of the mind." These things are good enough, no doubt, but what of the religion of the heart, which is after all the only religion there is — if the heart is the earthly representative of the soul? There are some people — fewer than is generally supposed — who really do not believe in the existence of the soul. Let me tell them that they are very near to denying the existence of the heart. Perhaps some of them do, and they may live to repent of their unbelief in this world, if not in the next.

What is the heart, or, rather, what do we in common conversation and writing understand by that word? It looks a great deal like attempting to define belief, but belief has received an excellent definition, for belief is knowledge and nothing else, so far as the individual who holds it is concerned. What we call the heart in each man and woman seems to mean the whole body of innate and inherited instincts, impulses, and beliefs, taken together, and in that relation to one another in which they stand after they have been acted upon throughout the individual's life by the inward vicissitudes and the

outward circumstances to which he has
been exposed.   When all this is quies-
cent I think we call it Self.   When
roused to emotional activity we call it
the Heart.   But whatever we call it,
it is to this Self or Heart that everything which is ethic and therefore permanent must appeal.

The foundation of good fiction and
good poetry seems to be ethic rather
than æsthetic.   Everything in either
which appeals to the taste, that is, to
the æsthetic side, may ultimately per-
ish as a mere matter of fashion; but
that which speaks to man as man, independently of his fashions, his habits,
and his tastes, must live and find a hearing with humanity so long as humanity
is human.   The right understanding of

men and women leads to the right re-
lations of men and women, and in this
way, if in any, a novel may do good;
when written to attain this end, it may
live; when addressed to the constant
element in human nature, it has as
good a right and as good a chance of
pleasing the men and women of the
world in our day, as it had to appeal to
the intellect of Pericles or to thrill the
delicate sensibilities of Aspasia. Their
novels were plays in outward effect, as
ours should be in inward substance,
and we must needs confess that the
form in which their intellectual artistic
luxuries were presented to them was
superior to that of the modern effort
included in four hundred pages at one
dollar and twenty-five cents. Possibly,

even probably, it is unfair to us to compare ourselves with Sophocles, Euripides, and Aristophanes; yet the comparison suggests itself if the definition be true and if our novels really aspire to be plays.

We have indeed something in our favour which the genuine playwright has not. We appeal entirely to the imagination, and, unless we use algebraic *formulæ* or scientific discussion, we give no standard measure in our books by which to judge the whole. We can call up surroundings which never were and never can be possible in the world, and if we are able to do it well enough we can put impossible characters upon our stage and make them do impossible things, and the whole,

acting upon a predisposed imagination, may create for the moment something almost like belief in the mind of
the reader. We can conceive a tale
fantastic beyond the bounds of proba-
bility, and if there be a touch of nature
in it, we may for a while transport our
readers into Fairyland. We can clothe
all of this in poetic language if our
command of the English tongue be
equal to the occasion, and we can lend
pathos to a monster and heroism to
a burlesque man. But the writer of
plays for the real theatre cannot do
this; if he does, he makes that which
in theatrical language is called a "burlesque" or a "spectacle"; or, if he be
a follower of the "decadent school,"
he may produce what he has decided

to call by a new name — a production
not always conducive to a high belief
in human nature.

The writer of plays, if he write them
for actual performance, has living
interpreters, and they and he are
judged by the standards of real life.
He is to a great extent dependent upon
his actors for the effect he hopes to
produce, and they are dependent not
only upon him, upon their individual
education, depth of feeling, and power
of expression, but also upon the material conditions and surroundings in which
they have to do their work. The most
dramatic scene of real life, if it actually
took place on the stage of a theatre,
would seem a very dull and tame affair
to any one who chanced to find him-

self in the body of the house. The
fundamental lack of interest, until it
has been artificially aroused, is a gulf
not to be bridged by such simple means
as being really "natural." The art of
the actor lies in knowing the precise
degree of exaggeration necessary to
produce the impression that he is not
exaggerating at all — but exaggeration
there must be. Without it, neither the
words nor the actions can speak or
appeal to the intelligence of the spec-
tator.

But we novelists are in an easier
position in our relation to our audience. We are granted many privileges
and have many advantages which the
playwright has not ; for we can appeal
to the heart almost directly without

the conscious intervention of practised eyes and ears, used to realities and eager to judge by real standards. We speak of Edwin's great height, broad shoulders, noble features and silken moustache, and are not obliged to look out for an actor who shall fulfil these conditions of manly beauty before we can be heard without being ridiculous. Angelina's heavy hair is a fact on paper; on the stage it is a wig, and must be a good one. Her liquid blue eyes are blue because we say they are; but it would annoy a playwright to find that his leading actress had light gray ones, when Edwin must compare them to the depths of the blackest night.

ALL this is rather frivolous, perhaps ;
but a little frivolity is to the point
here, since there can be no amusement
without a dash of it, and we profess to
provide diversion to meet the public
demand. With most men who have
moulded, hacked, and chiselled the
world into history, to think has been
to act. With us novelists, so far as
the world need know us, to think is
to dream, and perhaps to dream only
little dreams of merely passing significance. Few novelists are poets ; only
one or two have been statesmen ; none
have been conquerors. I suppose we
are very insignificant figures compared

with the great ones of this earth ; but
to our comfort we may dream, and if
we need consolation we may console
ourselves, as Montaigne puts it, with
the art which small souls have to interest great ones, "*L'art qu'ont les
petites âmes d'intéresser les grandes.*"

Frivolity is not weakness, though in
excess it may be a weakness. "*Carpe
diem*" is a good motto for the morning,
but in the evening "*Dulce desipere in
loco*" is not to be despised as a piece
of advice. The frivolities of great men
and famous women have filled volumes
of memoirs, and are not without interest to the little, as our little interests
do not always seem dull to the great.
The greater men are, the more heart
they have, good or bad, and the easier

it is to affect them through it, through
the multiform feelings which their
varied lives have created within them,
or through the few strong sentiments
by which most of them are ruled,
guided, or impelled according as they
are conscientious, calculating, or im-
pulsive, and to some extent according
to their nationality, a matter which has
almost as much to do with the author's
dream as with the reader's subjective
interpretation of it, and which largely
determines the balance between sentiment and sentimentality.

Sentiment heightens the value of
works of fiction as sentimentality lowers
it. Sentimentality is to sentiment as
sensuality to passion. The distinction
is not a fine one and has grown common

enough in our day to be universally understood. We owe it, I think, to the international balance of sentiment and sentimentality that the novelists of the present day are the French, Anglo-Saxons, and Russians. With all due respect to the great German intelligence, it does not seem capable of producing what we call a novel though it turns out most excellent plays. The German mind, measured by our standard, is sentimental, not romantic. Perhaps there is as much romance to be found in the history and traditions of Germany up to a date which I should place at about forty years ago as there is anywhere in the civilised world. Yet for some reason or other, the modern German, as I have said, seems to be more sentimental than romantic in his habits of thought and feeling.

It is not possible in a paper of this length to inquire into the foundations of sentimentality and romance. Practically, however, what we call a romantic life is one full of romantic incidents which come unsought, as the natural consequence and result of a man's or a woman's character. It is therefore necessarily an exceptional life, and as such should have exceptional interest for the majority. When our lives are not filled with emotions, they are too often crammed with insignificant details too insignificant to bear recording in a novel, but yet making up for each of us all the significance life has. The great emotions are not every-day phenomena, and it is the desire to experience them vicariously which creates the demand for fiction and thereby and at the same time a demand for emotion. This is felt more particularly nowadays than formerly.

There was a great deal of artificiality in the last century, and I believe very little real emotion or true sentiment. The evidences of the truth of this statement appear sufficiently, I think, in the current literature, the music, and the social manners of that time. Of the three the music alone has survived. Musicians constitute, in a certain sense, a caste, not unlike the Christian priesthood or the Buddhist brotherhood. Their art is more distinctly handed down from teacher to scholar, from master to pupil, than any other, and this may perhaps account for their unwillingness to break through their traditions and accepted rules. Few persons, however, can listen to an average symphony for orchestra, or sonata for piano, especially to the *allegro* movements, without being struck by the utter conventionality and artificiality of many parts of the production. This, it seems to me, is not due to the instinct of the musician, nor to the taste of the musical public, but is a distinct survival of a former existence, as much as the caudal appendage or the buttons on the backs of our coats. This is probably rank heresy from the musical point of view, and, like all I say here, is a mere personal opinion; but to judge by analogy from the remains of other arts cultivated a hundred years ago, there seems to be some foundation for it. Can any one see such plays acted, for instance, as Sheridan's, without being forcibly struck by the total absence of spontaneity and the absolute submission to social routine of the average society man and woman of those days. Sheridan's comedies are undoubtedly as true to their times on the one hand as they are to human nature on the other, but the humanity of them is thrown into vivid and strong relief by the artificiality of the elements in the midst of which the chief actors have their being. As for the literature, it is hardly necessary for me to defend the statement that it was conventional.

There was an intellectual dress, as it were, put on by the man of genius of those times. It hung loosely upon Goldsmith's irregular frame. It sat close, well-fitting and fashionable upon Addison, but Samuel Johnson's mighty limbs almost burst its seams and betrayed at every movement the giant who wore it. On a sudden the fashion changed, and it has not done changing yet.

The French Revolution seems to have introduced an emotional phase into social history, and to it we must attribute directly or indirectly many of our present tastes and fashions. With it began the novel in France. With it the novel in the English language made a fresh start and assumed a new form.

To take a very simple view of the question, I should like to hazard, as a guess, the theory that when the world had lived at a very high pressure during the French Revolution, the wars of Napoleon, and what has been called the "awakening of the peoples," it had acquired permanently "the emotional habit," just as a man who takes opium or morphia cannot do without the one or the other. There was a general desire felt to go on experiencing without dangerous consequences those varying conditions of hope, fear, disappointment and triumph in which the whole world's nervous system had thrilled daily during so many years and at such fearful cost. The children of the women who had gone to the scaffold with Marie Antoinette, the sons of the men who had charged with Murat, who had stood by La Tour d'Auvergne, or who had fired their parting shot with Ney, were not satisfied to dwell in returning peace and reviving prosperity with nothing but insipid tales of shepherds and shepherdesses to amuse them. They wanted sterner, rougher stuff. They created a demand, and it was forthwith supplied, and their children and children's children have followed their progenitors' footsteps in war and have adopted their tastes in peace.

MODERN civilisation, too, has done
what it could to stir the hearts of
men.   Evil communications corrupt
good manners, and it is not a play
upon words to say that the increased
facility of actual communications has
widened and deepened those channels
of communication which are evil, and
increased at the same time the demand
for all sorts of emotion, bad or good.
Not that emotion of itself is bad.   It
is often the contrary.   Even the mo-
mentary reflection of true love is a
good thing in itself.   It is good that
men and women should realise that a
great affection is, or can be, a reality

to many as well as a convenient amusement or a heart-rending drama to a
few.

Modern civilisation has created modern vices, modern crimes, modern virtues, austerities, and generosities. The
crimes of to-day were not dreamed of
a hundred years ago, any more than
the sublimity of the good deeds done
in our time to remedy our time's mis-
takes. And between the angel and
the beast of this ending century lie
great multitudes of ever-shifting, ever-
changing lives, neither very bad nor
very good, but in all cases very differ-
ent from what lives used to be in the
good old days when time meant time
and not money. There, too, in that
vast land of mediocrities, emotions

play a part of which our grandfathers
never heard, and being real, of the living, and of superior interest to those
who feel them, reflect themselves in
the novel of to-day, diverting the course
of true love into very tortuous channels and varying the tale that is ever
young with features that are often new.
Within a short few months I myself
have lived in a land where modern
means of communication are not, and
I have come to live here, where applied
science is doing her best to eliminate
distance as a factor from the equation
of exchanges, financial and intellectual.
The difference between the manifesta-
tions of human feeling in Southern
Italy and North America is greater
and wider than can be explained in

intelligible terms. Yet it is but skin-
deep. Sentiment, sentimentality, taste,
fashion, daily speech, acquired science,
and transmitted tradition cleanse, soil,
model, or deface the changing shell of
mutable mortality, and nothing which
appeals to that shell alone can have
permanent life ; but the prime impulses of the heart are, broadly speaking, the same in all ages and almost
in all races. The brave man's beats
as strongly in battle to-day, the cow-
ard's stands as suddenly still in the
face of danger, boys and girls still play
with love, men and women still suffer
for love, and the old still warn youth
and manhood against love's snares —
all that and much more comes from
depths not reached by civilisations nor

changed by fashions. Those deep
waters the real novel must fathom,
sounding the tide-stream of passion
and bringing up such treasures as lie
far below and out of sight — out of
reach of the individual in most cases
— until the art of the story-teller makes
him feel that they are or might be his.
Cæsar commanded his legionaries to
strike at the face. Humanity, the novelist's master, bids him strike only at
the heart.

THE END